Down on the Farm

BEES

Sally Morgan

QEB Publishing

QEB

Library of Congress Control Number: 2007001486

ISBN 978 1 59566 386 3

Written by Sally Morgan
Designed by Tara Frese
Editor Corrine Ochiltree
Picture Researcher Nic Dean
Illustrations by Chris Davidson

Publisher Steve Evans
Creative Director Zeta Davies
Senior Editor Hannah Ray

Printed and bound in China

Picture credits

CONTENTS

Words in **bold** can be found in the Glossary on page 22.

Bees on the farm

Do you know where **honey** and **beeswax** come from? They are both made by busy, buzzing honeybees.

Honeybees are **insects**. They live in places where there are many flowers. Farmers and gardeners like bees because they carry **pollen** from one flower to another. This helps the flowers make seeds.

4

Beekeepers keep their bees in beehives, like these.

Bees live together in groups called **colonies**. **Beekeepers** are people who look after bees. They build a **hive** for the bees to live in. Most beekeepers look after one or two hives, but some look after many more.

5

Bees from top to tail

Three types of honeybees live in a hive. Most are **worker bees**. These are the bees you see buzzing between flowers. A worker bee has a hairy body around ½ in. (1–1.5 cm) long. It has two pairs of see-through wings and an orange and black striped body.

Hairy body

Eye

Wings

Antenna

Legs

Sting

This large queen bee is surrounded by worker bees.

Height of a six-year-old child   Height of a beehive

The largest bee in a hive is the **queen** bee. There is only one queen bee in each hive and she is in charge. Male honeybees are called **drones**. There are hundreds of drones living in each hive.

7

It's a bee's life...

The queen bee lays her eggs in the hive. After three days, an egg hatches into a **larva**. The larva is white and has no wings. Worker bees feed the larva with bee bread. This is a mixture of honey and pollen.

Larvae look a bit like wiggly maggots.

After four days, the larva turns into a **pupa**. It stops moving while its body changes into an adult bee.

This baby bee used to be a larva.

Some larvae are given special food to eat, called royal jelly. The worker bees make it in their mouths. Larvae who are fed royal jelly turn into new queens.

Most worker bees live for about six to seven weeks. Drones live for about two months. A queen bee can live for up to two years.

Flower friends

Each day, honeybees leave the hive and fly around looking for flowers. They drink the sugary **nectar** made by many flowers.

Flowers produce pollen, too. This looks like yellow dust. Bees put the pollen into special baskets on their legs. They then take the pollen and nectar back to their hive.

This honeybee has collected a lot of pollen in its leg basket.

Bees are very useful little insects because they help make flowers grow. They carry pollen from one flower to another. It's an important job! Flowers need pollen to make seeds for new flowers.

Yummy honey

Inside the hive, worker bees chew the sugary nectar and pollen to make it into honey. The bees eat some honey and beekeepers collect the rest. They strain the honey to remove any beeswax and then put it into jars to sell.

As much as 154 lbs. (70 kg) of honey can be collected from one hive in a year. That's about the same weight as a grown-up man!

This beekeeper is removing a comb from the hive.

FARM FACT
Honey can be used to treat wounds. It stops germs from getting into the wound and helps it heal more quickly.

Honey varies in color from almost black to white. It can have a strong or mild taste. It all depends on the types of flowers the bees have visited. Honey made from heather flowers has a smoky taste.

Living in a hive

As many as 50,000 honeybees may live in a hive at a time. That's a lot of bees! Inside the hive, the bees use beeswax to build a **comb**. Each comb is made up of thousands of tiny, six-sided holes, called cells.

When they check their hives, beekeepers wear special clothes so that they do not get stung.

In summer, the beekeepers place the hives near to lots of flowers. At the end of summer, they remove some of the combs to collect the honey that has been stored inside. In winter months, when there are few flowers, the beekeepers feed the bees a sugary food, called candy.

15

Bees around the world

KILLER HONEYBEES

The Africanized honeybee is a cross between the honeybee from Europe and the African honeybee. It is found in South America. It has been nicknamed the killer bee because it is a fierce bee that will chase a person more than 109 yd. (100 m) to sting them. Run!

GIANT HONEYBEE

This wild bee is found in Asia and grows up to $3/4$ in. (15 mm) long. It makes its nest in trees and on cliffs. Beekeepers don't keep giant honeybees because they're not very friendly. They will sting a person without any reason.

DWARF HONEYBEE

This mini bee is only 0.3 in. (8 mm) long. That's tiny! It lives in southern parts of Asia and is a wild bee. Instead of living in a hive, this honeybee attaches its combs to tree branches.

17

Bee customs

ANCIENT EGYPT

Honey was very valuable in Ancient Egypt. It was used like money. One hundred pots of honey were enough to buy an ox or a donkey.

GREECE

In Greece, it used to be **traditional** for a bride to dip her finger into a pot of honey and make a sign of the cross before entering her new home. People believed it would bring the bride good luck.

ALL OVER THE WORLD

In many parts of the world, honey is part of Jewish New Year celebrations. Part of the celebration involves dipping slices of apple into honey. This brings good luck for the coming year.

19

Make a buzzy bee

Making your own honeybee is great fun and very easy. All you need is an egg carton, scissors, masking tape, paintbrushes and paints, crayons, pipe cleaners, glue, clear tape, and a plant stick.

1 Cut out two egg cups from the egg carton and stick them together with tape to make an oval shape.

2 Paint the body of the bee. Don't forget that bees have striped bodies!

3 Cut out a small circle from the egg carton and stick it on the front of your bee to make the head. Use your crayons to draw on big, buggy eyes.

4 Cut short lengths of pipe cleaner. Stick them onto your bee to make legs and antennae. Bend two more pipe cleaners to make wings, and stick them onto your bee.

5 Make a small hole in the underside of the bee and push the stick into it. Pop your bee in a vase of flowers.

21

Glossary and Index

antenna (plural antennae) feelers on an insect's body used to touch and feel things

beekeeper a person who looks after bees

beeswax a waxy substance made by bees

colonies large groups of bees that live together

comb a place where honeybees store honey in a beehive

drone the name given to a male honeybee

hive the place where honeybees live

honey a sugary substance made by bees

insects small animals with six legs and usually, wings

larva (plural larvae) the name given to the young of an insect. A larva hatches from an egg

nectar the sugary liquid made by some flowers

pollen the yellow "dust" made by a flower

pupa the stage in the life of an insect during which the body of the larva changes into the adult insect

queen the female honeybee that lays eggs

traditional a custom or way of doing something that is passed from parent to child

worker bees a type of bee that lives in the hive and collects nectar and pollen from flowers

Ideas for teachers and parents

- Watch honeybees at work in a garden or park. Make a note of the flowers the bees visit. Watch how the bees work their way around a flower. Make sure the children do not get too close to the bees, so they do not get stung!

- Look for some interesting recipes that use honey. Make them with the children, then see what they taste like.

- Ask a local beekeeper if it is possible to see inside a hive. Often, local beekeeper associations have open days for members of the public.

- Make a collage of honeybees. Take a large piece of white paper and draw outlines of bees on it, along with some flowers. Look through old magazines and cut out any pictures of bees and flowers. Stick these inside the outlines to make a colorful collage.

- Make a word search using the bee-related vocabulary in this book.

- Encourage the children to think of jokes and stories about bees. See if they can write a poem or a short story about a honeybee.

- Carry out a simple experiment to see which colors bees prefer. Place three small circles of colored paper (red, yellow, and blue) on the ground near a flower bed and place a little sugar water in the middle of each circle. Stand back and watch which color card the bees prefer.

- There are many different types of honey on sale at the store. Ask the children to look at the labels to see what type of flowers were used by the bees to make the honey. Some are made by bees visiting one type of flower, for example, heather or lavender. It is also possible to buy honey made by rain forest bees. Buy a couple of the different types of honey and do a taste test with the children.

PLEASE NOTE

Check that each child does not have any food intolerances before carrying out the honey recipes and the taste test.